GOD IS WITHIN HER: A

30-DAY DEVOTIONAL FOR

WOMEN

SHE WILL NOT FALL – STRENGTH

AND STILLNESS FOR EVERY SEASON

D.S. HOPE

INTRODUCTION

Dear Sister,

You picked up this devotional for a reason—maybe out of desperation, maybe out of curiosity, or maybe just because something in your heart whispered, *"I need more."* Whatever brought you here, know this: **God has been drawing you all along**.

This devotional was written for the woman who is walking through joy and sorrow, strength and struggle, peace and pressure. It's for the woman who knows God is real but sometimes forgets how to rest in Him. It's for the one who wants to stand firm, even when everything feels unsteady.

Over the next 30 days, you'll be reminded of what is already true: **God is within you. You will not fall.** His promises are not fragile. His presence is not far. Whether you're in a season of flourishing or just trying to keep going, He is right here—with grace for today and strength for tomorrow.

Each day invites you into a moment of quiet—a breath, a pause, a holy whisper. Let it speak to your heart. Let it carry you deeper. Let it remind you that your story matters, your soul is seen, and you are loved more than you know.

Welcome to this sacred journey of stillness and strength.

I'm honored to walk it with you.

With love,

D.S. Hope

1

UNSHAKABLE

Psalm 46

"God is within her; she will not fall; God will help her at break of day." — Psalm 46:5 (ESV)

Some mornings you wake up already weary. Before your feet hit the ground, your heart feels heavy and the world feels too loud. Maybe it's the tension in your home, the silence of unanswered prayers, or the fear of what lies ahead. It's easy to believe you're one small thing away from falling apart.

But then God whispers truth into your soul: *You are not alone, and you are not empty.* His presence isn't something you have to earn—it's already there. You carry Him with you. The world may tremble, but you won't. Not because you're fearless, but because you are **filled**. You are not running on your own strength today. You are walking with God *inside* of you.

When Psalm 46 says, *"God is within her,"* it's not poetic fluff—it's divine reality. He is closer than breath. He strengthens from the inside out. And because He is within you, you will not fall. You may cry. You may feel tired. But you will not break. Because He will help you at the break of day—right when you think the darkness has won, light rises.

You don't need to have all the answers today. You don't need to fix everything or be everything. You just need to remember who is within you. That's your anchor. That's your edge. You are unshakable, not because life is easy, but because **you are never alone in it**.

WHISPERS FROM THE FATHER

My daughter, I am not watching from afar—I am within you. You don't need to prove your strength. You need only to lean into Mine. When your knees are weak, I am your steadiness. When your heart trembles, I am your calm. You will not fall—I have declared it.

An Invitation to Reflect

- Where in your life do you feel most unstable right now?
- What would change if you truly believed God is already within you?
- How would you move through this day differently?

Prayer

Lord,

You are the strength that holds me steady. When everything feels uncertain, You are my certainty. Help me to rest in the truth that I am not alone and I am not fragile—I am filled with the presence of the Almighty. Teach me to walk in stillness and strength today.

Amen.

ADDITIONAL SCRIPTURE READINGS

- Isaiah 26:3 – *"You keep him in perfect peace whose mind is stayed on you..."*
- 2 Corinthians 4:8–9 – *"We are hard pressed on every side... but not destroyed."*
- Proverbs 31:25 – *"She is clothed with strength and dignity..."*

2

STILL WATERS

Psalm 23

"He makes me lie down in green
pastures. He leads me beside still
waters." — Psalm 23:2 (ESV)

There's something sacred about stillness. In a world where everyone rushes to be seen, to be heard, to be productive, stillness feels unnatural—almost like failure. But God calls us to it. Not as a punishment, but as a gift. Like a Shepherd who knows when His sheep are exhausted, He gently guides us to soft grass and quiet streams—not to accomplish more, but to *rest.*

You weren't made to run forever. You were made to pause. To breathe deeply. To lay your heart down beside still waters and remember that you are not the Shepherd. You don't have to make the path. You don't have to fix what's broken. You only need to follow the One who does.

Still waters don't mean a storm-free life. They mean *peace in the middle of the journey.* They remind you that God leads with gentleness, not force. He doesn't drive you like a taskmaster—He leads you like a Father who knows you need rest. He knows how tired your spirit can grow even when your calendar is full and your hands are busy doing "good things."

This kind of stillness doesn't come from external quiet. It's born inside—a settled soul that says, *Even now, God is near. Even now, He restores me.* And when He makes you lie down, it's not a sign of weakness. It's a sign of love. He makes you rest because He knows what's ahead. And He wants you ready—not burnt out, not empty, but **restored and steady.**

So let Him lead you today—not into striving, but into stillness.

WHISPERS FROM THE FATHER

Come, daughter. Sit with Me. Let the world hurry on—I am not in a rush with you. You are not behind. You are not forgotten. I will restore your soul beside these still waters. Breathe deeply. I am your peace.

An Invitation to Reflect

- Where in your life are you rushing past God's invitation to rest?
- What would it look like today to accept His stillness as a gift, not a disruption?
- Is your soul thirsty for the quiet voice of your Shepherd?

Prayer

Father,

Lead me beside still waters. Quiet the noise in my heart and in my mind. Help me to trust that I don't need to keep pushing to be worthy. Let me find my identity in You—not in what I do, but in who I am as Your daughter. Thank You for being a Shepherd who brings rest, not pressure.

Amen.

ADDITIONAL SCRIPTURE READINGS

- Matthew 11:28 – *"Come to me, all who labor and are heavy laden, and I will give you rest."*
- Isaiah 40:11 – *"He will tend His flock like a shepherd..."*

- John 14:27 – *"Peace I leave with you; My peace I give to you."*

3

MADE FOR THIS

Esther 4

"And who knows whether you have not
come to the kingdom for such a time as
this?" — Esther 4:14 (ESV)

There are moments in life when the weight
feels too heavy, when you question your place,
your purpose, your ability to keep going. You
might look around and think someone else
would be better suited—someone bolder,
someone braver, someone more qualified. But
God doesn't make mistakes in placement. He
doesn't overlook details. If you are here, now,

facing this moment—it's because **He placed you here**.

Esther was not a warrior. She wasn't trained in strategy or leadership. She was an orphan girl turned queen—reluctant, unsure, and aware of her limitations. And yet, through her, God rescued a nation. Not because she was fearless, but because she said *yes*. And in her yes, heaven moved.

You may not be standing in a palace, but you are standing in a purpose. The daily things—comforting a child, staying faithful in a struggling marriage, speaking life into a friend's storm, showing up at a job that tests you—these are not small. They are sacred. You are made for this, not because you feel strong enough, but because **God is with you in it.**

Every challenge in your path has already been filtered through His grace. You are not where you are by accident. Whether your season is quiet or chaotic, filled with tears or laughter, God is using it. And He is using *you*. You are part of His plan to bring light into darkness, peace into conflict, and hope into despair.

Don't minimize your moment. Don't despise the weight. This season might just be the very one He will use to show you how much He can do with a willing heart.

WHISPERS FROM THE FATHER

You don't have to be fearless, daughter—just faithful. I placed you here with purpose, with care, and with full awareness of your heart. Trust Me with your weakness. I will make you strong in the places you feel most unsure. You were made for this.

AN INVITATION TO REflECT

- What situation in your life feels too big for you right now?
- How does knowing God placed you here on purpose change the way you see it?
- What's one area where you need to trade fear for faith?

PRAYER

God,

Sometimes I doubt myself. Sometimes I question why I'm here, why You've allowed certain things, or why I feel so inadequate. But I trust You. Remind me that You don't make mistakes. Give me courage to be faithful in the middle of uncertainty. Let me say yes to You, even when I feel small.

Amen.

ADDITIONAL SCRIPTURE READINGS

- Jeremiah 1:5 – *"Before I formed you in the womb I knew you..."*

- 2 Corinthians 12:9 – *"My grace is sufficient for you..."*

- Romans 8:28 – *"...for those who love God all things work together for good..."*

4

Hidden, Not Forgotten

Genesis 16

"You are the God who sees me." —

Genesis 16:13 (NIV)

There are seasons where you feel unseen. You show up, you serve, you stay faithful—and yet it feels like no one notices. The prayers are quiet, the sacrifices are invisible, and the loneliness sinks deeper with each passing day. It's easy to wonder: *Does anyone see me? Does anyone care?*

Hagar knew that feeling. Cast aside, mistreated, and wandering in the wilderness with nothing but confusion and pain. She wasn't part of the plan, not in the way others were. She didn't hold power, and she wasn't praised. But in the middle of her running, in the middle of her despair, **God found her**. Not with a lecture, but with a question: *"Where have you come from, and where are you going?"*

He already knew the answer—but He asked so she would know that she mattered. That her story was not forgotten. That her tears were not wasted. And in that wilderness, Hagar gave God a name: *El Roi—The God Who Sees Me.*

You may feel hidden right now. You may be giving so much and receiving so little. But you are **not** forgotten. You are seen by the One who formed you. He sees the late-night prayers, the unsaid worries, the smile you give even when your heart is breaking. And He draws near.

God is not waiting to celebrate you when you "arrive" at some destination. He is celebrating your heart today—in the quiet, in the ordinary, in the behind-the-scenes obedience. You don't have to fight to be seen. You already are.

WHISPERS FROM THE FATHER

I see you, daughter. I see the moments you think no one else does. I see your tears, your giving, your trying. You are not lost in the crowd. You are held in My hands. I am the God who sees you, and I have never looked away.

An Invitation to Reflect

- Are there areas in your life where you feel unseen or overlooked?
- How does knowing God sees you change the way you walk through this season?
- What would it look like to rest in His approval instead of seeking others' recognition?

Prayer

God,

Sometimes I feel invisible. Sometimes I wonder if any of this matters. Thank You for reminding me that You see everything, even the things no one else does. Help me to trust that being seen by You is more than enough. Fill my heart with Your nearness.

Amen.

ADDITIONAL SCRIPTURE READINGS

- Psalm 139:1–3 – *"You have searched me, Lord, and You know me."*
- Matthew 6:6 – *"Your Father, who sees what is done in secret..."*
- Isaiah 49:15 – *"I will not forget you!"*

5

Rooted

Jeremiah 17

"She will be like a tree planted by the water that sends out its roots by the stream..." — Jeremiah 17:8 (NIV)

There is a quiet strength in the life of a tree. It doesn't rush. It doesn't strain to grow taller or reach wider. It simply sinks its roots deep and trusts the soil to nourish it, the sun to warm it, and the water to sustain it. And when the winds come—and they always do—it stands. Not because the storm is easy, but because the roots are deep.

You were made to live like that tree.

God never promised a storm-free life. He promised that when your life is *planted in Him,* you will endure. You may bend, but you will not break. The winds of anxiety, the droughts of disappointment, the pressure of expectation—they may press hard against you. But your strength is not in your branches. It's in your roots.

The world will tempt you to spread yourself thin. To chase what's flashy. To compare your bloom to hers. But the ones who last—the women who bear fruit in every season—are those who choose to stay planted. Steady.

Nourished by Living Water. Rooted in truth, not trends. Rooted in the Word, not the world.

You don't need to prove your growth. You don't need to be in bloom every season. Sometimes the most beautiful thing you can do is **remain**, trusting that what God is doing beneath the surface matters just as much as what anyone can see.

Sink deep today, daughter. Let your soul stretch down into His presence. And when the storm comes—and it will—you will not be shaken.

WHISPERS FROM THE FATHER

Stay close to Me, daughter. Let your roots grow deep in My Word, in My promises, in My presence. You don't have to chase what I've already given you. I will sustain you. I will grow you. Stay planted. I will bring the fruit in its season.

AN INVITATION TO REflECT

- Are your roots deep in God's Word, or stretched thin by distraction and comparison?
- What would it look like to intentionally stay planted this week?
- In what area of your life do you need to trust that growth is still happening beneath the surface?

PRAYER

Lord,

Help me to be like the tree You described—planted, steady, nourished. I don't want to be blown around by fear or comparison. Sink my roots deep into You. Teach me to trust the unseen work You're doing in me. I want to remain close and draw strength only from You.

Amen.

ADDITIONAL SCRIPTURE READINGS

- Psalm 1:3 – *"...like a tree planted by streams of water..."*
- Colossians 2:7 – *"Rooted and built up in Him..."*

- John 15:4 – *"Remain in me, as I also remain in you."*

6

LIFTED

Isaiah 46

*"I have made you and I will carry you; I
will sustain you and I will rescue you." —*

Isaiah 46:4 (NIV)

Some days feel too heavy to walk through. The
burdens you carry—some seen, some
secret—wear on your shoulders and settle deep
in your bones. You try to hold it together for
others. You smile when you're breaking. You
pray quietly because you don't even know how

to put the ache into words. And in those moments, strength feels far away.

But God speaks directly to the weary woman. *I have made you, and I will carry you.* Not, "I might," not "if you're strong enough"—but **I will**. He who formed you in your mother's womb doesn't ask you to carry the weight alone. He lifts it from you. And sometimes, when you can't walk at all, He lifts *you*.

God's love is not distant or theoretical. It is near. It is strong. It is deeply personal. And it shows up in the wilderness, in the long wait, in the place where you feel like you've run out of energy, answers, and reasons. He doesn't just sustain you when you're put together. He carries you when you're coming undone.

Even if no one else sees how hard you're trying, He does. He knows the burdens you carry and the ones you've laid down for everyone else. He doesn't rush you to recover or shame you for needing rest. He simply opens His arms and offers to carry it all—including you.

Let yourself be lifted today. Not because you're weak, but because you are **loved**.

WHISPERS FROM THE FATHER

I see how heavy it feels, daughter. Let Me lift it. Let Me lift you. You were never meant to carry this alone. I have held you from the beginning, and I will hold you now. Let Me be your strength. You don't have to earn My help—you only have to lean.

AN INVITATION TO REflECT

- What burden are you trying to carry in your own strength?
- Where might God be inviting you to rest in His arms instead of striving on your own?
- Are you willing to let Him lift you—even if you're used to being the strong one?

PRAYER

Father,

Thank You for seeing me and carrying me when I'm tired. I don't want to pretend I'm strong enough on my own anymore. I give You the weight I've been holding. Carry me through this season, Lord. Be my strength, my steadiness, and my rest.

Amen.

ADDITIONAL SCRIPTURE READINGS

- Deuteronomy 1:31 – *"...the Lord your God carried you, as a father carries his son..."*
- Psalm 55:22 – *"Cast your cares on the Lord and He will sustain you..."*
- Matthew 11:28 – *"Come to Me, all who are weary and burdened..."*

7

HELD IN THE STORM

Mark 4

"He got up, rebuked the wind and said to the waves, 'Quiet! Be still!' Then the wind died down and it was completely calm."

— *Mark 4:39 (NIV)*

The storm didn't wake Jesus—but the cry of His disciples did. As the boat rocked, as the waves rose higher and fear took hold, Jesus slept. Not because He didn't care, but because **He wasn't afraid**. And when they cried out, panicked and desperate, He stood and spoke peace into the chaos. Three words changed everything: *"Quiet. Be still."*

There are storms in your life that you didn't ask for. Sudden changes, deep disappointments, silent seasons where the noise around you feels unbearable. And maybe, like the disciples, you've wondered if God is sleeping through it all. If He sees the waves. If He hears your voice.

He does.

God doesn't panic like we do. He doesn't rush in fear. But that doesn't mean He's absent. It means He's sovereign. He sees the end from the beginning. And when the time is right, **He speaks peace**—not just over the storm, but into your heart. Sometimes He calms the winds, and other times, He holds you steady through them.

The beauty of this story isn't just that the storm stopped. It's that they were never alone in the boat. The One who commands creation was already in the middle of their fear, already present in their distress. That's the promise you carry today—you are **never** in the storm alone.

You don't have to calm the chaos. You just have to cry out to the One who can. And even if the waves keep crashing, you are held.

WHISPERS FROM THE FATHER

I'm here, daughter. I always have been. Though the storm rages, you are not alone. I am in your boat. I am not afraid. You don't have to fix it. Just come to Me, and I will speak peace over your fear. I will quiet your heart even before I quiet the wind.

An Invitation to Reflect

- What storm are you walking through right now—emotionally, spiritually, or physically?
- Have you mistaken God's silence for absence?
- What would change if you truly believed He is in the boat with you?

Prayer

Jesus,

You see the storm around me, and You see the one inside me too. I admit I've felt afraid and wondered if You were near. Remind me that You're always in the boat—that I am never alone. Speak peace to my heart. Calm what You will, and carry me through the rest.

Amen.

ADDITIONAL SCRIPTURE READINGS

- Psalm 107:29 – *"He stilled the storm to a whisper; the waves of the sea were hushed."*
- Isaiah 43:2 – *"When you pass through the waters, I will be with you..."*

- Philippians 4:7 – *"...the peace of God... will guard your hearts and your minds..."*

8

GRACE FOR TODAY

Matthew 6

"Therefore do not worry about tomorrow, for tomorrow will worry about itself. Each day has enough trouble of its own." — Matthew 6:34 (NIV)

Worry loves to live in the future. It imagines everything that could go wrong, everything that might fall apart. It writes stories in your mind that haven't happened yet but still steal your peace now. But Jesus invites you to stay here—in *today*—because that's where grace lives.

God doesn't give you tomorrow's strength today. He gives you *today's grace for today's needs*. Like manna in the wilderness, His provision comes fresh each morning. Just enough. Always enough. Not for your whole month, not for your entire future—but for this breath, this hour, this moment.

It's not easy to let go of the questions: *What if this doesn't work out? What if I'm not enough? What if I fail?* But peace isn't found in figuring everything out. Peace is found in trusting the One who already knows. He holds tomorrow, and He holds you. That's enough.

Today, God is offering you rest. Not in a change of circumstances, but in the quiet confidence that He is with you, **right now**. You don't need to run ahead. You don't need to control every outcome. You just need to breathe, release, and receive the grace He's pouring out—moment by moment.

If you only have the strength to do today, that's okay. You weren't meant to carry it all. Stay in this moment with your Shepherd. Tomorrow will come, and with it, new grace.

WHISPERS FROM THE FATHER

Daughter, you don't need to carry what hasn't happened yet. I am already there. But right now, I am here—with you. I've given you everything you need for today. Let go of tomorrow. Breathe deep. My grace is enough.

An Invitation to Reflect

- What worries about tomorrow are stealing your peace today?
- In what area is God asking you to trust Him with just one step instead of the whole path?
- How can you live more fully in the grace of this moment?

Prayer

Lord,

I confess—I carry tomorrow's weight as if it's mine to hold. Teach me to trust You with the unknown. Help me release the future and rest in the grace You've given me for today. Remind me that You are enough, here and now.

Amen.

ADDITIONAL SCRIPTURE READINGS

- Lamentations 3:22–23 – *"His mercies... are new every morning."*

- Exodus 16:4 – *"...I will rain down bread from heaven for you each day..."*

- Psalm 68:19 – *"Praise be to the Lord, who daily bears our burdens..."*

9

RADIANT

Psalm 34

"Those who look to Him are radiant;

their faces are never covered with

shame." — Psalm 34:5 (NIV)

There's a glow that doesn't come from makeup, good lighting, or a perfect life. It comes from looking up—especially when life is anything but easy. It's the radiance of a woman who, even through tears, keeps turning her eyes toward the One who loves her most.

The world will try to tell you your worth is in your appearance, your accomplishments, your ability to hold it all together. But God sees something deeper. He sees the light in your eyes when you trust Him in the storm. He sees the soft courage in your heart when you choose kindness over fear. That's the glow He gives—one that shines from the inside out.

This verse doesn't say the radiant woman has no struggles. It says that she looks to Him—*and that is what makes her shine.* Not shame, not striving, not self-sufficiency, but the simple act of looking to God in the middle of her reality.

Your light isn't in what others say about you. It's in the reflection of His face on yours. The more you turn your gaze to Him, the more you begin to reflect His peace, His joy, His gentleness. And that kind of beauty never fades. It can't be stolen. It doesn't depend on your season or your status. It's rooted in the God who lifts your head and removes your shame.

So lift your eyes today—not because everything is perfect, but because **He is**. You are radiant when you look to Him.

WHISPERS FROM THE FATHER

Daughter, look at Me. Don't let shame lower your head. Don't let fear steal your light. My face shines upon you, and My love restores your joy. You are radiant, not because of what you've done, but because you're Mine.

AN INVITATION TO REflECT

- Are you trying to find your worth in the wrong places?
- What would it look like to reflect God's light instead of chasing the world's approval?
- Where is God inviting you to lift your eyes today?

PRAYER

God,

Sometimes I forget where my beauty comes from. I chase approval. I cover shame. I compare and strive. But You remind me that I shine when I simply look to You. Lift my eyes. Let me reflect Your grace and goodness. Make me radiant with Your love.

Amen.

ADDITIONAL SCRIPTURE READINGS

- Numbers 6:25 – *"The Lord make His face shine upon you..."*
- Isaiah 60:1 – *"Arise, shine, for your light has come..."*
- 2 Corinthians 3:18 – *"...being transformed into His image with ever-increasing glory..."*

10

QUIET CONfiDENCE

Isaiah 30

"In quietness and trust is your strength..." — Isaiah 30:15 (NIV)

The world often shouts that strength is loud, bold, and constantly in motion. But God speaks a different kind of strength over His daughters—one that doesn't demand attention, but dwells in peace. **Quiet confidence** is not weakness. It's power under control. It's the heart that knows who her God is, so she doesn't have to prove who she is.

There's a holy hush in the soul of a woman who trusts the Lord. She doesn't panic when things shift. She doesn't chase what isn't hers. She waits. She listens. She leans into the still, small voice that others often miss. Her strength isn't measured in noise but in *knowing*—knowing that God is able, that He is near, that she is not forgotten.

Sometimes the bravest thing you can do is not react. Sometimes real faith looks like pausing when everything in you wants to fight or flee. Quiet confidence is courage wrapped in humility. It's the kind of beauty that endures when the showy strength of the world fades away.

You don't have to be the loudest voice in the room to carry authority. You don't need to shout to be heard by God. He honors the woman who trusts quietly, who stays close when she doesn't understand, who holds peace even when the world is shaking.

Let today be marked not by striving, but by stillness. Not by proving, but by **resting in who God says you are**.

WHISPERS FROM THE FATHER

> I am your strength, daughter—not your words, not your image, not your defense. You don't have to shout to be strong. You only need to trust Me. I will fight for you. I will

go before you. Let quiet confidence
be your robe today—I delight in it.

AN INVITATION TO REflECT

- Where are you tempted to prove your
  strength or worth right now?
- What would it look like to step back and
  let quiet trust lead instead?
- How has God shown Himself strong in
  your silence before?

PRAYER

Father,

Help me rest in You. When I want to rush,
defend, or control, remind me that true
strength is found in quiet trust. Teach me to

wait without fear and to move only when You lead. Let my heart grow still and confident in Your unshakable goodness.

Amen.

ADDITIONAL SCRIPTURE READINGS

- Exodus 14:14 – *"The Lord will fight for you; you need only to be still."*
- Psalm 131:2 – *"I have calmed and quieted my soul..."*
- Proverbs 17:27 – *"...a person of understanding is even-tempered."*

11

RESTORED

Joel 2

"I will restore to you the years that the swarming locust has eaten..." — Joel 2:25 (ESV)

There are seasons that feel wasted. Years marked by pain, silence, or regret. Moments when your heart aches at all that was lost—time you can't get back, opportunities that slipped away, relationships that broke, or choices you wish you could undo. But God is not only a Redeemer—He is a **Restorer**. And what feels too broken for you is never beyond His healing hands.

In Joel's time, the locusts had devoured everything. Fields were stripped bare, and hope was hard to come by. But God spoke a promise to His people—not just of healing, but of restoration. He didn't say, "I'll give you something new to make up for the old." He said, *"I will give you back what was lost."* That's His heart for you, too.

God can restore time, joy, dreams, and even parts of your soul that you thought were too damaged to feel again. What the enemy meant to destroy, God can use to rebuild something stronger, something more beautiful. He does not waste anything—not even your wilderness.

Restoration doesn't always look like going back. Sometimes it looks like something new growing out of the ashes. Sometimes it's the deep healing that comes in your spirit, the peace you thought you'd never find again. And sometimes, it's the quiet assurance that **nothing is ever truly lost when it's placed in God's hands**.

You are not beyond restoration. Your story is not over. The God who restores the years is still writing new pages for you—pages filled with beauty, grace, and joy.

WHISPERS FROM THE FATHER

I see what was taken, and I know how it hurt. Nothing you've lost is beyond My reach. I will restore what was broken, redeem what was wasted, and renew what you thought was gone forever. I'm not finished. I never stopped loving you. Trust Me to rebuild.

AN INVITATION TO REflECT

- What season or loss in your life feels wasted or beyond repair?
- Can you surrender that part of your story to the God who restores?
- What new thing might God be doing even now in the place that once felt barren?

PRAYER

Lord,

You are the Restorer of all things. I bring You the broken years, the hurts I've buried, and the hope I've let go of. Thank You for not wasting anything. Teach me to trust that You can bring beauty from ashes and healing from loss. Restore me in the deepest places.

Amen.

ADDITIONAL SCRIPTURE READINGS

- Isaiah 61:3 – *"...to bestow on them a crown of beauty instead of ashes..."*
- Psalm 71:20 – *"You will restore my life again..."*

- Romans 8:28 – *"...in all things God works for the good of those who love Him..."*

12

ENOUGH

2 Corinthians 12

"My grace is sufficient for you, for My power is made perfect in weakness." — 2 Corinthians 12:9 (NIV)

There's a quiet pressure that weighs heavy on many women—the pressure to be enough. Enough for your family, your job, your calling. Enough to handle the pain, the plans, the pace. You pour yourself out and wonder if what you gave even made a difference. You try to hold it together while quietly unraveling inside.

But the truth is this: **you were never meant to be enough on your own**. That was never the expectation. God doesn't call you to perfection—He calls you to dependence. His grace meets you where your strength ends. Not to shame your weakness, but to shine His power through it.

Paul, the apostle, pleaded with God to remove the thing that made him feel weak. But instead of taking it away, God answered with a promise: *My grace is sufficient*. Not lacking. Not almost. But **completely enough**.

God's grace isn't a backup plan. It's the plan. It carries you when your confidence falters. It covers you when your energy runs out. It fills the cracks left by fear, fatigue, and failure. And it whispers the truth the world forgets to tell you: *You are not enough—but He is. And because He lives in you, you are held, you are loved, and you are covered.*

So today, release the pressure. Lay down the lie that says you must be everything. You only need to be His—and He is more than enough for every place you feel lacking.

WHISPERS FROM THE FATHER

You don't have to strive, daughter. You don't have to prove. I see you. I know what you carry, and I know where you feel small. But I am enough for you. My grace is your strength. Rest in Me. You are safe here.

AN INVITATION TO REflECT

- Where are you trying to be "enough" in your own strength?
- How can you release that burden and rely on God's sufficiency instead?
- What would your life look like if you truly believed His grace is enough for you?

PRAYER

Father,

Thank You that I don't have to be everything. Thank You that You are more than enough.

Teach me to rest in Your grace instead of performing for approval. Fill every place in me that feels empty. Be my sufficiency today.

Amen.

ADDITIONAL SCRIPTURE READINGS

- Psalm 73:26 – *"My flesh and my heart may fail, but God is the strength of my heart..."*
- Philippians 4:13 – *"I can do all things through Christ who strengthens me."*
- John 1:16 – *"From His fullness we have all received grace upon grace."*

13

CHOSEN

1 Peter 2

"But you are a chosen people, a royal priesthood, a holy nation, God's special possession..." — 1 Peter 2:9 (NIV)

There's a pain that comes from feeling overlooked. From being the one passed by, the one who didn't get picked, the one who always seems just outside the circle. You may smile and go about your day, but deep down, the question lingers: *Am I truly wanted? Am I really seen?*

But God speaks directly to that ache. *You are chosen.* Not by accident. Not as an afterthought. But on purpose, with love, and with full knowledge of every part of who you are. He didn't choose you for your perfection—He chose you because He loves you. Completely. Personally.

Being chosen by God means you belong—even when others reject you. It means you have purpose—even when your life feels ordinary. It means that your identity is not based on what the world says about you, but on what your Creator declares: *You are Mine.*

You don't have to earn a seat at His table. He's already set a place for you. You don't have to chase approval or compete for attention. You are already fully known, fully loved, and fully accepted in Him.

Today, let this truth settle deep in your soul: **you are not invisible, and you are not random. You are chosen, royal, holy, and treasured.** And nothing—no mistake, no season, no opinion—can undo that.

WHISPERS FROM THE FATHER

I chose you. Before the world knew your name, I called you Mine. You don't need to strive for what I've already given. You belong. You are wanted. You are set apart. Walk in that truth, daughter. Let it shape how you see yourself today.

An Invitation to Reflect

- In what area of your life have you felt overlooked or unwanted?

- How would your mindset shift if you truly believed you are chosen and set apart by God?

- What would change if you lived today like someone who is deeply wanted by the King?

Prayer

Lord,

Thank You for choosing me. When I feel forgotten, help me remember that I am always known by You. When I doubt my worth, remind me that You have called me special, royal, and Yours. Let this truth shape my heart and my identity today.

Amen.

ADDITIONAL SCRIPTURE READINGS

- Ephesians 1:4 – *"He chose us in Him before the creation of the world..."*
- Deuteronomy 7:6 – *"The Lord your God has chosen you out of all the peoples..."*
- John 15:16 – *"You did not choose Me, but I chose you..."*

14

WAITING WELL

Lamentations 3

"The Lord is good to those who wait for Him, to the soul who seeks Him. It is good that one should wait quietly for the salvation of the Lord." — Lamentations 3:25–26 (ESV)

Waiting is never easy. It stretches the soul. It quiets the noise and leaves you face to face with your questions, your hopes, and sometimes your doubts. Whether you're waiting for healing, for direction, for a child, for restoration, or simply for clarity—it can feel like a sacred ache that only heaven understands.

In the stillness of waiting, you're tempted to believe that God is distant or unconcerned. But waiting isn't punishment—it's preparation. It's the space where roots grow deeper, where trust is tested and strengthened, and where faith shifts from theory to reality. It's the place where you stop striving and start resting—not in your own timeline, but in God's perfect timing.

To wait well isn't to wait passively. It's to wait *expectantly*. To seek God in the quiet. To stay close when you don't feel anything changing. To believe that even now, even here, **God is**

working behind the scenes with love and precision. And when the breakthrough comes, it will not be rushed. It will be right.

Your waiting season is not a wasted season. It's a holy one. It's where transformation is happening—not just around you, but within you. So be still. Breathe deep. Your soul is safe in His hands, and His goodness will meet you in time.

WHISPERS FROM THE FATHER

I see you waiting, daughter. I know the weight you carry and the prayers you whisper in the dark. I'm not late. I'm preparing the answer and preparing your heart. Trust My

timing. I have not forgotten you.
You are in the middle of My love,
even now.

An Invitation to Reflect

- What are you waiting for in this season
  of your life?
- How can you shift from waiting
  impatiently to waiting with trust?
- What has God already taught you in this
  place of pause?

Prayer

God,

Waiting is hard. Some days it feels like nothing
is happening and my heart grows weary. But I

choose to trust You. Help me to wait well—not with anxiety, but with hope. Strengthen my faith in the silence. Let me believe You are working even when I cannot see it.

Amen.

ADDITIONAL SCRIPTURE READINGS

- Psalm 27:14 – *"Wait for the Lord; be strong, and let your heart take courage..."*

- Isaiah 64:4 – *"No eye has seen a God besides You, who acts for those who wait for Him."*

- Romans 8:25 – *"If we hope for what we do not yet have, we wait for it patiently."*

15

OVERflOWING

Romans 15

"May the God of hope fill you with all joy

and peace as you trust in Him, so that

you may overflow with hope by the

power of the Holy Spirit." — Romans

15:13 (NIV)

Some days you feel empty—like you're pouring out more than you're receiving, stretching further than your soul feels able to go. The kind of tired that sleep doesn't fix. The kind of ache that sits quietly under the surface. You give and serve and smile, and somewhere along the way, you wonder: *Is there anything left in me?*

But the God you serve is not a God of scarcity. He is the God of **overflow**. He doesn't just trickle grace into your life—He fills. He doesn't just offer enough peace to get by—He multiplies it. And He doesn't just hand out drops of hope—He causes it to **abound**.

This kind of life doesn't come from doing more. It comes from *trusting more*. As you rest in Him, as you lean into His promises, He begins to fill the parts of you that have run dry. And when He fills you, it never stops at the brim. It spills over. Into your relationships. Into your mindset. Into your worship. Into the places that once felt barren and lifeless.

God doesn't ask you to manufacture joy or fake peace. He asks you to draw near to Him. He is the Source. And when your life is connected to the Source, **your soul begins to overflow**—not with your own strength, but with His.

Today, if you feel poured out, let Him pour back in. He's not looking for performance. He's looking for surrender. And He's ready to fill you with more than enough.

WHISPERS FROM THE FATHER

Come to Me, daughter. Let Me be your Source again. You don't have to keep pushing from an empty place. I have joy for your sorrow, peace for your worry, and hope that never runs dry. Let Me fill you—and then let it overflow.

An Invitation to Reflect

- Where in your life do you feel emotionally or spiritually empty?
- Have you been trying to pour out without allowing God to pour into you?
- What would it look like to trust Him today and receive His fullness?

Prayer

Lord,

I come to You tired, stretched, and needing more of You. Fill me again. Fill me with joy where there's been heaviness, peace where there's been anxiety, and hope where there's been discouragement. I can't live poured out without first being filled by You.

Amen.

ADDITIONAL SCRIPTURE READINGS

- John 7:38 – *"Whoever believes in Me... rivers of living water will flow from within them."*
- Psalm 23:5 – *"...my cup overflows."*
- Philippians 1:11 – *"...filled with the fruit of righteousness that comes through Jesus Christ..."*

16

SILENT STRENGTH

1 Peter 3

"Your beauty should not come from outward adornment... rather, it should be that of your inner self, the unfading beauty of a gentle and quiet spirit, which is of great worth in God's sight." — 1 Peter 3:3–4 (NIV)

There's a strength that doesn't raise its voice. It doesn't need to be loud or forceful. It isn't defined by dominance, but by deep inner peace. It's the strength of a woman who knows who she is in Christ—and doesn't need to prove it to anyone.

This kind of strength isn't always seen from the outside. It shows up in the woman who chooses to pray instead of argue. Who keeps showing up when no one claps. Who speaks kindly even when she's misunderstood. Who forgives when it would be easier to harden her heart. This is not weakness. This is **power clothed in gentleness**.

The world may not reward this kind of spirit, but God treasures it. He sees the quiet battles you fight, the grace you extend when it costs you, the way you choose love over control. And He calls it beautiful—**unfading beauty** that doesn't depend on seasons or circumstances.

You don't have to shout to be heard by heaven. You don't have to be loud to be bold. Sometimes the strongest women are the ones who live surrendered, steady, and rooted in peace. The ones who carry quiet confidence, not because they're certain of themselves, but because they're certain of their God.

So today, walk softly, but carry the strength of the Spirit within you. The world may not always notice—but heaven does.

WHISPERS FROM THE FATHER

I see your quiet strength, daughter. I see the gentleness the world overlooks, and I call it precious. You don't need to be loud to be powerful. Your peace speaks volumes. Let My Spirit strengthen you in stillness. You are radiant in your softness.

An Invitation to Reflect

- Where have you equated strength with being loud, reactive, or in control?
- How have you seen God work through quiet strength in your life or someone else's?
- What would it look like to embody gentleness as a form of courage?

Prayer

Lord,

Make me strong in the ways that truly matter. Help me to value a gentle and quiet spirit even when the world sees it as small. Fill me with Your peace, Your patience, and Your grace. Let me be a woman of silent strength—powerful, yet surrendered.

Amen.

ADDITIONAL SCRIPTURE READINGS

- Proverbs 31:25 – *"She is clothed with strength and dignity..."*
- Isaiah 32:17 – *"The fruit of righteousness will be peace..."*
- Colossians 3:12 – *"Clothe yourselves with compassion, kindness, humility..."*

17

RENEWED

Isaiah 40

"But those who hope in the Lord will renew their strength. They will soar on wings like eagles; they will run and not grow weary, they will walk and not be faint." — Isaiah 40:31 (NIV)

There are seasons when you're just trying to make it through the day. You run on empty, push through the tired, and keep going because you don't feel like you have a choice. And yet, somewhere deep in your spirit, you long for more than just survival—you long for **renewal**.

This promise from Isaiah isn't about never getting tired. It's about what happens *after* you've come to the end of yourself. God's strength doesn't show up in the absence of weariness—it meets you in it. It breathes new life into tired bones. It lifts you when you feel too heavy to rise on your own.

To be renewed doesn't mean to go back to who you were before the trial. It means to become stronger through it. It's a holy rebuilding. A gentle restoration. And it begins when you stop trying to outrun your weakness and start anchoring your hope in the Lord instead.

When you wait on God—not passively, but with expectation—He doesn't just refill you. He transforms you. And suddenly, you find yourself rising. Not always soaring, but **rising**. Because your strength is no longer your own. You are carried by something greater.

You may feel slow, worn, or behind today. But heaven is not in a hurry. And your renewal is coming. Breathe. Wait. Hope. And rise.

WHISPERS FROM THE FATHER

Come to Me, weary one. I will renew you. I will lift you. I will breathe strength back into the places that feel dry and worn. You were never meant to carry this

alone. Let Me be your rest. Let Me
be your wings.

An Invitation to Reflect

- Where are you running on empty
  today—physically, emotionally,
  spiritually?
- What would it look like to pause and
  wait on God instead of pushing forward
  in your own strength?
- Can you trust that God is not only
  refilling you, but reshaping you?

Prayer

Father,

I'm tired. I've been carrying more than I know how to hold. But I come to You with open hands and an open heart. Renew me. Fill me with Your strength. Help me to rise again—not by force, but by grace. Thank You for being my source of life.

Amen.

ADDITIONAL SCRIPTURE READINGS

- Psalm 23:3 – *"He restores my soul..."*
- 2 Corinthians 4:16 – *"Though outwardly we are wasting away, inwardly we are being renewed day by day."*

- Matthew 11:28 – *"Come to Me, all you who are weary and burdened, and I will give you rest."*

18

ANCHORED

Hebrews 6

"We have this hope as an anchor for the soul, firm and secure." — Hebrews 6:19 (NIV)

Hope can feel fragile when life keeps shifting beneath your feet. Plans unravel. People change. Emotions rise and fall. Some days, it feels like you're being tossed around by waves you didn't ask for and storms you didn't see coming. But there's a kind of hope that isn't built on what happens next—it's built on who God is. And that hope is your **anchor**.

Anchors don't keep storms away. They keep the boat from drifting when the storm hits. You're still going to feel the winds. You're still going to see the waves. But you will **not be moved**, because your soul is secured in something stronger than circumstances.

When your heart is anchored in Christ, you're not swayed by fear, disappointment, or uncertainty the same way. That doesn't mean you don't feel those things—it just means they don't define you. They don't drag you under. Because deeper than the chaos is a still point, a holy tether, and it holds you fast.

Maybe today your soul feels like it's drifting—trying to grab hold of something to keep you steady. Let it be Jesus. Not your performance, not your plan, not the approval of others—but **His promise**, which never moves and never breaks.

The waters may rise, but you are not adrift. Your hope is secure. You are held.

WHISPERS FROM THE FATHER

When the winds rise, I will hold you. When the waves roar, I will not let go. I am your Anchor, daughter—firm, steady, and near. You are not drifting. You are tethered to My heart. Let My promises be the place you rest.

An Invitation to Reflect

- In what area of your life do you feel unsteady or uncertain?
- What have you been anchoring your hope to—and has it held firm?
- How can you more intentionally anchor your heart in God's unchanging truth?

Prayer

Lord,

You are my Anchor. When everything else feels unsure, You are steady. Help me not to look for security in things that shift. Teach me to trust

Your promises and rest in Your strength. Keep my heart grounded in hope that holds.

Amen.

ADDITIONAL SCRIPTURE READINGS

- Psalm 62:6 – *"Truly He is my rock and my salvation; He is my fortress, I will not be shaken."*

- Isaiah 33:6 – *"He will be the sure foundation for your times..."*

- Colossians 1:23 – *"...continue in your faith, established and firm..."*

19

Unseen Battles

Exodus 14

"The Lord will fight for you; you need only to be still." — Exodus 14:14 (NIV)

Some battles aren't visible to anyone else. You carry them quietly—in your thoughts, in your body, in your relationships, in the private spaces of your soul. And the hardest part? Feeling like you have to keep fighting them alone.

But Scripture reminds us: **you're not alone in the battle.** Even when no one else sees what you're facing, God sees it all. And more than that—He is fighting for you.

When the Israelites stood with the Red Sea before them and Pharaoh's army behind them, there was nowhere to run. Panic rose, fear screamed, and logic said, *"This is the end."* But God said, *"Be still."* Not because they were doing nothing, but because **He was doing everything.**

Stillness is not weakness. It's the posture of trust. It's where you lay down the sword of control and let God go before you. It's how you stop swinging at shadows and start standing on promises.

God fights differently than we do. While we try to figure it all out, He's already made a way through the sea. While we brace for impact, He speaks peace over the chaos. He doesn't just defend you—**He delivers you**.

So today, whatever battle you're in—mental, emotional, spiritual—be still. Don't confuse silence with defeat. God is moving in the unseen, and victory is often born in surrender.

WHISPERS FROM THE FATHER

> You don't have to fight alone. I see the battle behind your smile. I know what weighs on your chest at night. I am with you, and I am fighting for you. Be still, daughter. I've got this—and I've got you.

AN INVITATION TO REflECT

- What unseen battles are you carrying right now?
- Have you been trying to fight in your own strength instead of trusting God?
- What would "being still" look like for you today?

PRAYER

God,

You see what I'm carrying—the battles no one else knows about. Thank You that I don't have to win them on my own. Teach me to be still, to trust, and to let You fight for me. I surrender the struggle into Your hands.

Amen.

ADDITIONAL SCRIPTURE READINGS

- 2 Chronicles 20:17 – *"You will not have to fight this battle… stand firm and see the deliverance the Lord will give you."*

- Psalm 34:7 – *"The angel of the Lord encamps around those who fear Him, and He delivers them."*

- Romans 8:31 – *"If God is for us, who can be against us?"*

20

FEARLESS

Joshua 1

"Have I not commanded you? Be strong and courageous. Do not be afraid; do not be discouraged, for the Lord your God will be with you wherever you go." —

Joshua 1:9 (NIV)

Fear whispers lies in the dark—*you're not ready, you're not enough, you'll fail, you'll fall.* It wraps its fingers around your heart, making even small steps feel overwhelming. And yet, over and over again, God says the same thing to

His daughters: **Do not be afraid. I am with you. Be courageous.**

Courage doesn't mean you don't feel fear. It means you don't let fear have the final word. When God called Joshua to lead a nation, the road ahead was full of unknowns, dangers, and giants. But God didn't hand him a plan—He gave him a **presence**. *"I will be with you wherever you go."* That promise is the same for you today.

You don't need to know the whole path to move forward. You only need to know the One who walks with you. Courage is born in those who believe that God's presence is greater than the threat, that His voice is louder than fear, and that **faith steps forward even when knees are shaking**.

Fear will always try to stop you—especially when you're on the edge of something meaningful. But you were not created to shrink back. You were created to rise, to trust, to walk in strength that doesn't come from you but flows through you.

So take the step. Say yes. Let go. Speak up. Whatever fear is trying to silence, bring it into the light. Because God is with you—and that makes you fearless.

WHISPERS FROM THE FATHER

I am with you, daughter. When fear rises, let My love cast it out. You are not alone in this. I will go before you and behind you. Be strong—not because of who you are, but because of who I AM. I made you brave.

AN INVITATION TO REflECT

- What has fear been keeping you from doing, saying, or believing?
- How would your mindset shift if you truly believed God is with you wherever you go?
- What step can you take today in faith, even if fear still lingers?

PRAYER

Father,

Fear tries to hold me back, but You have called me forward. Fill me with courage. Help me to trust You more than I fear the unknown. Thank You for being with me in every step. Today, I choose to walk by faith—not because I'm fearless, but because I'm never alone.

Amen.

ADDITIONAL SCRIPTURE READINGS

- Isaiah 41:10 – *"So do not fear, for I am with you..."*
- Psalm 56:3 – *"When I am afraid, I put my trust in You."*
- 2 Timothy 1:7 – *"For God gave us a spirit not of fear but of power..."*

21

LOVED DEEPLY

Romans 8

"For I am convinced that neither death
nor life... nor anything else in all
creation, will be able to separate us from
the love of God that is in Christ Jesus our
Lord." — Romans 8:38–39 (NIV)

Some days, love feels distant. Maybe because people have failed you. Maybe because you've failed yourself. Or maybe you've just been walking through a season that makes it hard to feel anything at all. But God's love is not a feeling. It's not a reward for getting everything right. It's a promise—a **deep, unwavering, always-and-forever kind of love**.

Nothing you've done has disqualified you from it. No mistake has put you outside its reach. No wound, no silence, no broken chapter can separate you from the love that chased you before you even knew you needed chasing.

Paul didn't write Romans 8 from a mountaintop. He knew suffering. He knew prison, rejection, uncertainty. And yet, he was convinced—*nothing* could separate us from the love of God in Christ. That means on your best days and your worst, in moments of great faith or deep fear, **you are held by a love that does not let go.**

God's love is not delicate. It doesn't flinch when you doubt. It doesn't fade when you're tired. It is deep and wide and fiercely present. And if you've ever wondered if you're truly lovable, remember this: **you are deeply loved—not because you are flawless, but because He is faithful.**

Let His love be the truth you return to today.

WHISPERS FROM THE FATHER

Nothing will ever separate you from My love. Not your fear. Not your failure. Not your feelings. I love you completely and eternally. You don't have to earn it. Just receive it. You are Mine, and I delight in you.

An Invitation to Reflect

- Are there parts of you that struggle to believe you are truly and deeply loved?

- What past pain or present lie may be standing in the way of receiving God's love?

- How would your life look different if you walked in the full confidence of being unconditionally loved?

Prayer

Lord,

Thank You for loving me with a love that never fails. Help me to receive it—not just in my mind, but deep in my heart. Tear down the walls I've built and the lies I've believed. Let Your love fill every broken space in me.

Amen.

ADDITIONAL SCRIPTURE READINGS

- Ephesians 3:17–19 – *"...to grasp how wide and long and high and deep is the love of Christ..."*
- Zephaniah 3:17 – *"He will take great delight in you... He will rejoice over you with singing."*
- John 15:9 – *"As the Father has loved Me, so have I loved you."*

22

JOY COMES IN THE MORNING

Psalm 30

"Weeping may stay for the night, but rejoicing comes in the morning." —

Psalm 30:5 (NIV)

There are nights that feel endless—nights of grief, heartbreak, uncertainty, or quiet battles where tears speak the words you can't find. You wonder if the heaviness will ever lift, if the morning will ever truly come. And while the sunrise doesn't always remove the pain, it does bring a promise: **this sorrow is not forever.**

God sees your night. Not just the outward struggles, but the deep, wordless ache inside. He is not a distant observer. He draws close. He holds you while you weep. He listens when all you can offer is silence. And He whispers hope even before the sky begins to lighten.

This verse is not a denial of pain—it's a declaration that **pain will not be the end of the story**. Weeping *may stay*—for a moment, a season, a stretch of time that feels longer than your heart can bear. But it *will not remain.* The morning will come. Joy will return. And it will be deeper, stronger, more radiant because of what you've walked through.

Sometimes, the joy comes softly. In laughter that returns like a timid guest. In peace that steadies your breathing. In a new beginning you didn't see coming. God doesn't just restore your joy—He redeems your sorrow. He makes beauty from ashes, not by erasing your story, but by gently writing something new.

Hold on through the night. The morning is on its way. And with it comes joy—not forced or fake, but real joy, born from the presence of the One who never left your side.

WHISPERS FROM THE FATHER

I see your tears, daughter. I hold every one. But know this—your night will not last forever. I am with you in it, and I am already preparing your morning. Joy is coming. Trust Me in the dark, and watch what I will bring with the light.

An Invitation to Reflect

- What sorrow or heaviness are you carrying today?
- Have you allowed yourself to grieve with God instead of hiding your pain from Him?
- Where might joy be quietly waiting to rise again in your life?

Prayer

Lord,

Some days the sorrow feels heavier than hope. But I believe You are the God of the morning. I trust that joy will return, even if I can't see it yet. Walk with me through the night. Hold my heart steady. Let Your light rise over my pain.

Amen.

ADDITIONAL SCRIPTURE READINGS

- Isaiah 61:3 – *"...a crown of beauty instead of ashes, the oil of joy instead of mourning..."*
- John 16:20 – *"...your grief will turn to joy."*
- Psalm 126:5 – *"Those who sow with tears will reap with songs of joy."*

23

WALKING ON WATER

Matthew 14

"Then Peter got down out of the boat,

walked on the water and came toward

Jesus." — Matthew 14:29 (NIV)

There comes a point in every woman's journey where faith calls her out of comfort. Where staying in the boat feels safer, but something inside her knows—*Jesus is out there, and she wants to be where He is.* That moment is holy. Risky. Terrifying. Beautiful.

Peter didn't walk on water because he had superhuman courage. He stepped out because he *saw Jesus* and believed Him more than the waves. But somewhere between the step and the shore, his eyes shifted. The wind howled. Fear crept in. He began to sink—not because Jesus moved, but because Peter did. Still, even in that sinking moment, Jesus reached out and held him.

That's grace.

You may be in a place where God is asking you to take a step. To trust Him in a way that makes no sense. To move when the ground under your feet feels more like water than rock. You may be afraid you'll fail. But hear this: **you are**

safer walking toward Jesus in the storm than sitting comfortably without Him.

Walking on water isn't about getting it perfect. It's about keeping your eyes on the One who doesn't sink. It's about believing that even if you fall, **His hand is already reaching for you**.

Don't let fear chain you to the boat. Let faith move your feet. Even shaky steps are still steps. And with Jesus, every step forward is a miracle in the making.

WHISPERS FROM THE FATHER

> Step out, daughter. Don't wait for the wind to die down—step out while it's still swirling. Keep your

eyes on Me. I won't let you drown. Even when your faith falters, My hand will hold you. Trust Me—miracles happen in motion.

An Invitation to Reflect

- Where is God calling you to step out in faith right now?
- What fears are keeping you in the boat?
- What would it look like to focus more on Jesus than on the waves?

Prayer

Jesus,

I want to walk with You—even when it feels uncertain. Help me to fix my eyes on You instead of my fears. Give me courage to step out, and faith to keep walking. And when I stumble, catch me with Your grace. I trust You.

Amen.

ADDITIONAL SCRIPTURE READINGS

- Proverbs 3:5–6 – *"Trust in the Lord with all your heart..."*
- Isaiah 43:2 – *"When you pass through the waters, I will be with you..."*
- Hebrews 12:2 – *"...fixing our eyes on Jesus, the pioneer and perfecter of faith..."*

24

LETTING GO

Proverbs 3

"Trust in the Lord with all your heart

and lean not on your own

understanding; in all your ways submit

to Him, and He will make your paths

straight." — Proverbs 3:5–6 (NIV)

Letting go sounds easy until it's your hands that have to release. The plans you've carefully mapped. The relationship you've poured yourself into. The control you've clung to just to feel safe. There's a part of you that wants to trust—but also a part that fears what might happen if you're no longer the one steering.

But God never asked you to understand everything. He simply asks you to **trust Him with everything**.

There's freedom that only comes on the other side of surrender. Not the kind that says "I give up," but the kind that says, "I give in—to Your will, to Your ways, to Your better plan." Because deep down, you know that His wisdom reaches farther than your vision, and His heart is always turned toward your good.

Letting go is holy. It's an act of worship. It's choosing to believe that even if things don't go according to your timeline or idea of success, **God will still lead you well**. He has not lost sight of you. He's already gone before you. And He knows the path that will bring peace, even when you can't see where it ends.

Today, open your hands. Release what you've been holding so tightly. Let the weight of control fall, and let the peace of trust rise in its place. You don't have to figure everything out—you just have to follow.

WHISPERS FROM THE FATHER

You don't have to hold it all together, daughter. I've never asked you to carry what I already offered to hold. Let go. Let Me lead. My path may be different from yours,

but it will always be for your good. I
will not fail you.

AN INVITATION TO REflECT

- What are you holding onto out of fear,
  pride, or self-protection?
- What would it feel like to place that fully
  into God's hands today?
- Can you trust that letting go is not
  losing—but gaining deeper peace?

PRAYER

God,

I've been trying to hold on, to figure things out,
to make things work. But I surrender. I choose
to trust You more than my own understanding.

Teach me to release what's not mine to control.

Lead me where You know I need to go.

Amen.

ADDITIONAL SCRIPTURE READINGS

- Psalm 37:5 – *"Commit your way to the Lord; trust in Him and He will do this."*
- Matthew 6:10 – *"Your will be done..."*
- Isaiah 55:8–9 – *"My thoughts are not your thoughts, neither are your ways My ways..."*

25

IN THE VALLEY

Psalm 23

"Even though I walk through the darkest valley, I will fear no evil, for You are with me; Your rod and Your staff, they comfort me." — Psalm 23:4 (NIV)

The valley is not where we want to be. It's shadowy, uncertain, and quiet in all the ways that make you feel exposed and alone. There's no fast forward button through the hard seasons—no detour around the grief, the confusion, the fear. But here's the hope: **you are not walking through it alone.**

Psalm 23 doesn't pretend the valley doesn't exist. It acknowledges it—fully and honestly. And then it delivers the promise: *God is with you there.* Not just waiting on the other side. Not just cheering you on from above. **With you. In it. Step by step. Breath by breath.**

Sometimes, in the valley, you learn things about God you could never see on the mountaintop. You learn how close He really is. How tender His voice sounds in the dark. How steady His hand feels when everything else is trembling. The valley doesn't define you—but it does shape you. It deepens your faith, strengthens your soul, and teaches you to lean into His comfort like never before.

God doesn't promise to remove every valley. But He does promise you won't walk a single one without Him. And His presence will be your peace, even when there's no explanation, no resolution, no map.

So if you're in a valley right now, keep walking. Don't pitch a tent in despair. Don't listen to the lie that God has left you. **He is closer than ever—and He's not letting go.**

WHISPERS FROM THE FATHER

I am walking with you through this, daughter. I know it's dark, but I am your light. I know it's lonely, but I

am near. Let My presence be your
comfort. You don't have to be
strong—I will carry you through the
valley. One step at a time.

AN INVITATION TO REflECT

- What "valley" are you currently walking
  through in your life?
- How have you seen God's presence in a
  painful or uncertain place?
- What would it mean to rest in His
  comfort instead of rushing to escape?

PRAYER

Lord,

This valley feels long, and I don't always know how to keep walking. But I believe You are with me. Help me to feel Your nearness. Be my comfort, my guide, and my strength. Even in the shadow, let me rest in Your light.

Amen.

ADDITIONAL SCRIPTURE READINGS

- Isaiah 41:13 – *"I am the Lord your God who takes hold of your right hand..."*
- John 16:33 – *"In this world you will have trouble. But take heart..."*
- Psalm 34:18 – *"The Lord is close to the brokenhearted..."*

26

HER YES MATTERS

Luke 1

"I am the Lord's servant," Mary

answered. "May your word to me be

fulfilled." — Luke 1:38 (NIV)

There's a quiet power in a woman's yes to God. Not because she knows all the answers. Not because she feels strong enough. But because she trusts the One who's asking. Mary didn't have a blueprint for what would happen next. She didn't have guarantees or reassurances that it would be easy. But she had faith. And she said yes.

That yes changed everything.

God still moves through women who surrender. Through the ones who don't wait to feel "ready" before stepping out in obedience. Through the ones who say yes while trembling. Through the ones who offer their ordinary lives for His extraordinary purposes. **Your yes may feel small—but in God's hands, it carries eternal weight.**

Your yes may look like forgiveness when you'd rather hold a grudge. It may look like staying when it would be easier to run. Starting something new. Letting something go. Believing again. Loving again. Trusting again.

Whatever it is—if God is leading, your yes matters more than you know.

Obedience doesn't require clarity. It just requires surrender. And surrender isn't weakness—it's the deepest form of strength. It says, *"I trust You more than I trust myself."* And that is the kind of yes that opens doors to miracles.

Say yes—even when it's hard. Even when it costs you. Even when you're afraid. Because every time you say yes to God, **you align your heart with His purpose—and that is where life truly begins.**

WHISPERS FROM THE FATHER

Your yes matters to Me, daughter. Even the quiet, uncertain one. I'm not asking you to be perfect—only willing. When you say yes, I move. I work. I bless. Trust Me. I will carry you through everything your yes brings.

An Invitation to Reflect

- What is God asking you to say yes to in this season?
- What fears or doubts have been holding you back from surrendering?
- How would your life change if you fully trusted Him with the outcome of your obedience?

PRAYER

Lord,

I want to say yes to You—even when I don't understand. Help me to trust You more than I fear the unknown. Give me courage to obey, even when my voice shakes. Use my yes for Your glory, and let Your will be done in me.

Amen.

ADDITIONAL SCRIPTURE READINGS

- Isaiah 6:8 – *"Here I am. Send me!"*
- Romans 12:1 – *"...offer your bodies as a living sacrifice..."*
- John 2:5 – *"Do whatever He tells you."*

27

SHIELDED

Psalm 18

"As for God, His way is perfect: The
Lord's word is flawless; He shields all
who take refuge in Him." — Psalm 18:30

(NIV)

There are days when life feels like a
battlefield—unexpected arrows of criticism,
waves of discouragement, whispers of fear. You
brace yourself, wondering how much more you
can take. But God hasn't left you exposed. He is

your **shield**—not just your comfort after the battle, but your protection *in* it.

A shield doesn't remove you from the fight. It stands between you and what's coming for you. It absorbs the impact, deflects the enemy's blows, and makes sure that even when you feel under attack, **you are never unguarded**.

When you take refuge in God, you're not hiding in weakness—you're standing in strength. His presence surrounds you. His promises defend you. His Word becomes your armor. And though life may throw its worst, it cannot break you, because the One who shields you **never sleeps and never fails**.

You don't have to be on constant guard. You don't have to live in fear, always bracing for the next wound. You can rest. Because your Defender is alert. His way is perfect. His protection is sure. And He has promised that whoever runs to Him will not be turned away.

So breathe deep today. You are not alone on this battlefield. You are covered. You are shielded. You are held close by the God who fights for you.

WHISPERS FROM THE FATHER

Stay close, daughter. Let Me be your shield. I see what's coming long before it reaches you. I will cover you. I will guard your heart and soul. You don't need to fear the

arrows—you only need to stay near
to Me.

An Invitation to Reflect

- What battles have left you feeling exposed, afraid, or worn down?
- In what ways can you take refuge in God instead of relying on your own strength?
- Are you willing to trust Him to protect what you can't control?

Prayer

Lord,

You are my shield—my refuge, my safe place. When I feel attacked or afraid, help me to run to You first. Cover me with Your presence.

Surround me with Your peace. Thank You for being my defender, even when I don't see the danger coming.

Amen.

ADDITIONAL SCRIPTURE READINGS

- Psalm 3:3 – *"But You, Lord, are a shield around me..."*
- Proverbs 30:5 – *"He is a shield to those who take refuge in Him."*
- Ephesians 6:16 – *"...take up the shield of faith..."*

28

FAITH THAT RISES

Mark 5

"He said to her, 'Daughter, your faith has
healed you. Go in peace and be freed
from your suffering.'" — Mark 5:34

(NIV)

She didn't have a name in the story, just a long
history of pain. Twelve years of bleeding.
Twelve years of isolation, of doctors, of
disappointment. And yet somehow—*she still
had faith.* Not loud or flashy, but just enough
to reach through a crowd and touch the edge of

His robe. Just enough to believe that **He could heal what no one else could fix**.

That's the kind of faith that rises.

It rises not because life is easy, but because the soul refuses to stop believing. It rises after years of heartbreak. It rises in the middle of the struggle. It rises with trembling hands and silent prayers. And Jesus doesn't overlook it. He honors it. He calls it beautiful. *"Daughter, your faith has healed you."*

Maybe your faith feels small today. Maybe it's buried under questions, fatigue, or past disappointments. But it's still there. Still alive. Still powerful. Because faith isn't about the size—it's about the direction. **If your faith is reaching for Jesus, it is enough.**

God is not measuring your faith against someone else's. He's not asking for perfection. He's simply asking you to believe—to reach, to trust, to keep coming close even when it hurts. Because the faith that rises doesn't need to be loud. It only needs to be real.

And when it reaches for Him, *He always responds*.

WHISPERS FROM THE FATHER

Even when your hope feels thin, even when your hands shake, I see your faith. I honor it. I bless it. Keep reaching for Me, daughter. I am here. I am healing. I am moved by your trust, even when it's quiet.

An Invitation to Reflect

- What have you stopped believing God for, out of fear or disappointment?
- Where is He inviting you to reach again—to hope again?
- How can you nurture even the smallest seed of faith in this season?

Prayer

Jesus,

My faith isn't perfect, but it's real. I believe You can heal what still hurts. I believe You see me, even when I feel unseen. Help my faith to rise again—not in my strength, but in Your power. I trust You with what feels impossible.

Amen.

ADDITIONAL SCRIPTURE READINGS

- Hebrews 11:1 – *"Now faith is confidence in what we hope for…"*
- Matthew 17:20 – *"…faith as small as a mustard seed…"*
- Psalm 34:4 – *"I sought the Lord, and He answered me…"*

29

BECOMING

James 1

"Let perseverance finish its work so that you may be mature and complete, not lacking anything." — James 1:4 (NIV)

We often crave arrival—the moment when we finally feel complete, healed, confident, "there." But the truth is, we are always in the process of **becoming**. And that process? It's rarely easy. It's marked by refining, stretching, and the uncomfortable middle between who we were and who we are becoming.

James reminds us that God is not just fixing us—He's finishing us. And He does it through perseverance. Through the days we choose faith over fear. Through the seasons when we keep going even when we don't feel strong. Through the hard places that teach us how deeply we can trust Him.

God is not impatient with your process. He's not disappointed that you're still learning, still struggling, still becoming. **He delights in the journey, because He walks every step with you.**

You are not behind. You are not broken beyond repair. You are clay in the hands of a loving Potter, and He knows what He's shaping—even when you don't. Every trial, every tear, every test is being used to form something holy in you. Something complete. Something beautiful.

So if today feels messy or incomplete, that's okay. God is not finished yet. And when He's the one doing the work, you can trust that the end result will be more than you imagined.

You are becoming. And He calls it good.

WHISPERS FROM THE FATHER

I see what you are becoming, even when you can't. I'm not rushing you. I'm not asking for perfection—only perseverance. Stay close to Me, and I will finish the work I started in you. You are already beautiful to Me, even now.

An Invitation to Reflect

- Where in your life do you feel stuck or incomplete?

- How can you shift your focus from performance to progress?

- What would it look like to trust God with the pace and shape of your becoming?

Prayer

God,

Thank You that I am a work in progress and not a finished product. Thank You that You are patient with me and faithful to complete what You've started. Help me to embrace the process—not with frustration, but with faith. Keep shaping me, Lord.

Amen.

ADDITIONAL SCRIPTURE READINGS

- Philippians 1:6 – "...*He who began a good work in you will carry it on to completion...*"
- Isaiah 64:8 – "*We are the clay, You are the potter...*"
- Romans 5:3–4 – "...*suffering produces perseverance; perseverance, character; and character, hope.*"

30

SHE WILL NOT FALL

Psalm 46

"God is within her, she will not fall; God will help her at break of day." — Psalm 46:5 (NIV)

You've been through valleys. You've faced storms. You've walked in seasons of waiting, letting go, breaking, rebuilding, becoming. And through it all, one truth has remained: **God has been within you the entire time**.

This journey hasn't been about perfection. It's been about presence—His, not yours. You were never meant to be unshakable in your own strength. You were meant to carry the strength of the One who lives within you. And that strength? It does not fail.

There will still be hard days. There will still be unknowns. But you can stand in the middle of it all and say with confidence, *"I will not fall."* Not because everything is perfect, but because **He is.** Not because you feel ready, but because **He is already here**—inside you, beside you, before you.

You are a woman held by grace. Strengthened by truth. Steadied by hope. And though you may bend, though you may weep, though you may question—**you will not fall.** Because God is your help. And He comes with mercy every morning and enough love to carry you through every night.

This is who you are now. A woman of stillness and strength. A daughter who knows she is not alone. A heart that may tremble, but will never be overcome.

WHISPERS FROM THE FATHER

You've made it, daughter. Not by your power, but by Mine. I have been with you through every step. And I will never stop being your strength. You will not fall—not now, not ever—for I am within you, and I will help you always.

AN INVITATION TO REflECT

- How has God revealed His presence to you during this devotional journey?
- What truth do you need to carry forward into your next season?
- How will you remind yourself that even when you feel shaken, you are never without Him?

PRAYER

God,

Thank You for walking with me. For holding me. For teaching me what it means to be a woman who does not fall—because You live within me. I surrender my fears, my future, and my heart to You again. Help me live rooted in Your strength every day.

Amen.

ADDITIONAL SCRIPTURE READINGS

- 2 Corinthians 4:8–9 – *"...persecuted, but not abandoned; struck down, but not destroyed."*

- Deuteronomy 31:6 – *"He will never leave you nor forsake you."*

- Psalm 121:3 – *"He will not let your foot slip..."*

Final Blessing

She Will Not Fall

Beloved daughter,

You have walked through thirty days of truth, and not one of them depended on your perfection—only your presence. You showed up. You listened. You opened your heart. And in doing so, you made space for the One who has always been there, quietly dwelling within you.

You are not the same woman who began this journey.

You have learned to rest, to rise, to reach, and to release. You've remembered what it means to be chosen, covered, and called. You've discovered that strength does not always roar—it often whispers, *"Still, I stand."* And now, you stand with the confidence that **God is within you, and you will not fall.**

May you walk forward with a steadiness that comes not from control, but from trust.

May your soul stay anchored in truth when the waves come.

May your voice carry grace, your hands carry peace, and your heart beat with the courage of the One who formed it.

May you never forget that your story is sacred, your journey is seen, and your yes still matters.

And when the world shakes, may you remember:

You are not alone. You are not lost. You are not going under.

You are a woman held by God.

Now go, in strength and in stillness.

Go in peace.

Go in love.

Go in the fullness of the One who is always within you.

Amen.

THANK YOU SO MUCH

Thank you for choosing *God Is Within Her: A 30-Day Devotional for Women*. I pray it met you in the moments you needed most and reminded you that you are never alone—God is with you, within you, and for you.

If this devotional blessed you in any way, I'd be so grateful if you would take a moment to leave a review on Amazon. Your kind words help other women discover this journey of strength and stillness—and every review truly makes a difference.

With love and gratitude,

D.S. Hope

Made in the USA
Monee, IL
12 June 2025